God With Us

A Family Advent Celebration

Written by Katie Pawlak

for Annie Grace and Karis Joy

God With Us: A Family Advent Celebration © 2014

This book is designed to make the celebration of Advent simple and memorable for the entire family. Daily readings corresponding with twenty-five symbols from the Old and New Testaments, short prayers, and extension activities provide a flexible and engaging approach to celebrating Advent for children ages 4-14, and the adults who love them.

The Jesse Tree is a Christmas tradition that traditionally takes place during the Advent season. In the days leading up to Christmas, a tree, banner, or branch is decorated with ornaments depicting symbols from stories in the Bible that point ahead to the lineage and birth of Christ, the long-awaited Messiah. This book uses the Jesse Tree format to celebrate God's enduring faithfulness to His people through the sending of His Son to earth that first Christmas night.

Gather your family to recount what God has done, who He has been, and who He still is to His people. As one generation "commends your works to another" (Ps. 145:4), you will find your attention rightly focused on God's magnificent gift to His people at Christmas –
Jesus Christ, Emmanuel, God with us.

Table of Contents

Suggestions for Use

This book is designed to be used as a family devotional. A story theme, Bible verses, reading, prayer, and extension activities are provided for the twenty-five days in December leading up to, and including, Christmas day. Opening the Bible together is a powerful activity for families, and you are encouraged to look up and read the verses listed under each day's heading before reading the devotional portion aloud. This can be an excellent time to model for your family how to look up verses in the Bible and to impart the relevance of scripture in our daily lives. At the same time, there are certain circumstances (reading with young children, for example) that may necessitate efficiency and for that reason you can find the daily verses listed in full in Appendix A.

You can choose to read only the scripture, devotional reading, and prayer. You may also decide to complete an extension activity or two to further engage with each day's story theme. Three "Branching Out" activities or questions are provided for each story theme, ranging in both complexity and depth. You know your family best and are invited to select activities that match the developmental stages and interests of your family.

This book may also be used in conjunction with ornaments that correspond to the daily verses and readings. The ornament symbols pictured in the back of this book can be cut out or color copied onto card stock and hung on a Christmas tree, branch, felt banner, or twine strung across the mantle. (Hand-embroidered felt and wooden ornaments matching the images in this book, as well as a printable file of the ornament images and other resources, are available for purchase online at www.katiepawlak.com)

The most important activity related to this book is coming together as a family and focusing your collective attention on God, and the gift of His Son, in the days leading up to Christmas. I pray this time becomes a treasured tradition in your family, as it has in ours.

December 1: *The Jesse Tree*

Isaiah 11:1-2

Long, long ago, there was a big problem. God's people had stopped trusting and obeying Him and their hearts were far from His. Like Adam and Eve in the garden of Eden, God's people thought they could find wisdom and happiness on their own, apart from God. They were forced to leave their homeland, and what used to be a great kingdom became a small group of wanderers. God, however, loved His people deeply and He made them a promise. He sent His messenger Isaiah to tell the people that God had a plan to send Someone who would save them from destruction. A man in Jesse's family would come with wisdom, power, and strength to lead God's people back to Him.

God's people waited a long time for their true King, Jesus, to be born. Advent is a season of waiting and remembering for us, too. The word "advent" means "coming." We get ready to celebrate Jesus' birth during Advent, when God came to earth in the form of a baby. We also remember that Jesus promises to come back again in glory to establish a kingdom of justice and peace; this is the second Advent. As we look forward to Christmas, we learn to be patient and to trust the plan God has for us. God shows His love and faithfulness to us over and over again as we remember what He has done and what He is still doing for His people.

Father in Heaven, thank You that You have a plan for Your people and for each one of us. Thank You for sending Jesus as a baby to become the Savior for each one of us. Help us to be patient and thankful as we look forward to celebrating Christmas.

Branching Out

1. What is your favorite part of the Christmas season?
2. How do we try to find happiness apart from God? Where do you think God wants us to find true happiness and wisdom?
3. Isaiah prophesied that a "branch" from Jesse's family tree would grow and bear fruit. If you have a copy of your family tree, ask someone in your family to show it to you. Ask them to tell you about your relatives. In what ways are you similar to or different from them?

December 2: *Creation*

Genesis 1:1, 27, 31

In the beginning, before the earth or people or plants or animals existed, there was only God. The Bible tells us that Jesus was God. He was with God when the world was created: "the Word was with God, and the Word was God. He was with God in the beginning" (John 1:1-2). The "Word" was another name for Jesus, God's Son. Togetherness was important to God from the very start.

God created the entire world – He spoke, and day and night, sky and ground, plants, animals, water, air, and people were created. The world was perfect when He created it, because God Himself is perfect. He loved everything He made with His whole heart. God created man and woman to be His close friends- to walk and talk and enjoy His creation together with Him. Adam and Eve, the first man and woman, loved talking with God. Their hearts were so full with His love and peace that there was no room for fear or sadness. They spent their days caring for the plants and animals God had placed in their garden home. God saw everything that He created and said that it was very good.

Creator God, thank You for making our world and everything in it. Fill our hearts with peace as we remember that You created us with Your perfect love.

Branching Out

1. Make a paper "earth": Color a coffee filter or paper towel with blue and green washable marker. Lightly spray with water, and watch the colors mix. Let it dry and display it somewhere special.
2. God created the world, and said that it was good. Talk about something you have made with your hands. It can be a drawing, art project, craft, food, or something entirely different. Would you call it good?
3. What does it mean to be created in the image of God?

December 3: *Adam and Eve*

Genesis 3:12-13   Isaiah 53:6

Adam and Eve, the first man and woman, lived closely with God. They spent their time talking with God and enjoying the world He created until one day when they disobeyed the instructions He gave them. God gave Adam and Eve permission to eat from any tree in the garden of Eden, except for the fruit from a specific tree in the middle of the garden. Instead of listening to God, they chose to listen to the evil serpent Satan and ate the fruit anyway. Eating the fruit and leaving the boundaries God created to keep them safe brought sin into God's perfect world.

Adam and Eve felt ashamed and hid from God. Their sin angered God, but God kept loving them. Still, God had to discipline Adam and Eve for disobeying. God sent Adam and Eve out of His beautiful garden as a consequence for their disobedience and to protect them from living forever in a world that was now stained by sin. Since the beginning of time, God's love for His people has been so strong that He can't stop loving us, even when we sin and wander away from Him like lost sheep. God made a plan for our sin to be forgiven and for our hearts to be fixed forever. He would send a Savior to His people to bring forgiveness for their sin and to redeem them back to a right relationship with Him.

Loving Father, we all sin by choosing our own way. Thank You for sending the Good Shepherd, Jesus, to lead us back to You.

Branching Out

1. Create an art project using an apple- cut an apple in half. Dip the cut side in a thin layer of paint and stamp onto a blank card or piece of paper. Talk about what happened when Adam and Eve disobeyed God and ate fruit from the tree in the garden of Eden.
2. Do you think you would have eaten the apple? Why or why not?
3. How do boundaries and instructions keep us safe? Talk about the guidelines your family has in place and how obeying them can protect you.

December 4: *Noah*

Genesis 6:17-19   Genesis 9:11-13

After Adam and Eve left God's garden, sin continued. Eventually, God's people were sinful all the time. God made a plan to get rid of the sin by sending a flood to destroy the earth and its people. He did this so He could start new with people who trusted Him.

Noah was a friend of God. God told Noah to make a big boat, called an ark, so that his family and two of every animal on earth and in the sky would be saved from the terrible flood. He gave Noah special instructions for building the ark. The people didn't believe Noah when he talked about the flood and their need to be rescued. They laughed at him, and when the rains started, they were destroyed along with all the plants and animals that were left on earth.

When the flood was over and the waters disappeared, God made a covenant with His people to never send a flood to destroy the earth again. A covenant is a special and sacred promise. God put a rainbow in the sky to remind the people of His special promise. He knew that when it rained again, God's people would need a beautiful reminder that He would never again destroy the earth with a flood. God's people would continue to choose sin, but He was working out a plan. Rather than destroying His people when their sin separated them from God, He would send a Savior to provide a way for their sin to be forgiven, and to flood their hearts with the hope of eternal life.

Gracious God, thank You for reminding us of Your promises. When we see a rainbow in the sky, help us to remember that You love us and that You sent Jesus to rescue us from sin.

 Branching Out

1. Color or paint a picture of a rainbow as a reminder of God's covenant promise to His people.
2. Talk about what it might have been like to be on a boat for 40 days with so many animals. What do you think it sounded like? Smelled like? Felt like?
3. The Bible says that Noah "walked with God" (Genesis 6:9). What does it look like to walk with God? Can you think of anyone else in the Bible who walked with God? (see Genesis 5:22, 24)

December 5: *Abraham*

Genesis 12:2   Genesis 15:5-6

Sometimes God asks us to do difficult things and it can be hard or uncomfortable to obey. A very long time ago, God asked a man named Abram to leave his home city and everything he knew and take a very long trip. God made many special promises to Abram. One of those promises was that Abram and his family would have a special blessing, even though he and his wife had no children at the time. After God made the special promise, He gave Abram and his wife Sarai new names- Abraham and Sarah. Abraham means "father of many peoples" and Sarah means "mother of nations."

Abraham was known for his great faith in God. Even though Abraham and his wife Sarah were very old, they believed God's sacred promise to them that they would have many descendants- so many that it would be impossible to count them all, just like the stars in the sky! When they were very old, God gave Abraham and Sarah a son named Isaac, and their descendants became the chosen people of God.

God kept every single one of His promises to Abraham and everyone on earth was blessed by his great faith. God promised to rescue the world through Abraham's family. One of his descendants would be the Perfect Savior, Jesus, who would fix our hearts for good and allow us to be made right with God forever.

Father God, thank You for sending a Savior through Abraham. Give us strength to obey You even if You ask us to do hard things. Help us to have a strong faith, like Abraham, that is a blessing to others.

 Branching Out

1. Before you go to bed tonight, go outside and look at the stars. Try to count them!
2. What does your name mean? What is special about the meaning of Abram and Sarai's new names?
3. Abraham is remembered as a man of great faith. Share about someone you know whose faith has blessed or encouraged you.

December 6: *Isaac*

Genesis 22:8-13

God needed to know that Abraham trusted Him completely in order to make sure His plan for rescuing His chosen people would work. God asked Abraham to do something very difficult to see if he would still obey Him. One day, God asked Abraham to give Him his only son, Isaac. Abraham's love for his son was strong but his love for God was even stronger. Together, he and his son carried the things they needed for offering a sacrifice to God up a tall mountain. Usually a lamb was killed and sacrificed on an altar when someone wanted to offer a sacrifice to God, but they did not bring a lamb with them. When they got near the top of the mountain, Isaac asked, "Where is the lamb?" (Genesis 22:7). Abraham trusted that God would provide a lamb for them, but they still had no lamb when they reached the mountaintop. Abraham tied Isaac's hands and feet together and got ready to sacrifice his son on the altar. At the right time, God sent an angel to stop him. God gave them what they needed at just the perfect moment- a ram to die in Isaac's place, which they found caught in a bush.

Years later, God would send someone else from Abraham's family to take our place - His only Son, Jesus, who would also be offered as a sacrifice by His Father, God. He would die in our place, for our sins, and He would be known as the Lamb of God (1 John 1:29, 36).

Merciful Father, thank You for protecting us and sending us just what we need at the perfect time. We honor Abraham's example of love for You. Thank You for giving Your own Son for us so we can live and be set free from our sins.

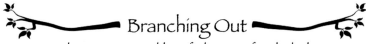

Branching Out

1. What object or person is most special to you? How would you feel or react if God asked you to give that up?
2. Act out this story with your family. Think about how Abraham may have felt as he walked up the hill with his son Isaac.
3. In this story, who speaks and who listens? What can we learn about trusting and obeying God from Abraham's example?

December 7: *Jacob*

Genesis 28:12-15

Jacob made many bad choices in his life. He was running away from some of those choices one day when God gave him a special dream. In the dream, God reminded Jacob of the special covenant promises He made to Abraham and Isaac, Jacob's grandfather and father. When Jacob woke up he knew God had spoken to him and shouted, "Surely, the Lord is in this place and I was not aware of it!" (Genesis 28:16).

The Lord reminded Jacob that even if he tried to run from his family, the wrong things he had done, and even from God Himself, he was never completely alone. God was always with Jacob and the promises God made to Jacob's ancestors were important for Jacob as well. God's big plans for Jacob and his family were not limited by Jacob's bad choices. Jacob made a special stone pillar to remember the promise-filled dream from God and he began to follow and obey God from that day forward. God reaffirmed to Jacob that one day all the people on earth would be blessed by his family. Because Jacob turned back to God and received His promise, another descendant of his family would come to be our true stairway or ladder to God. Jesus came to be the bridge between us and God so we can know God and His promise of eternal life.

Forgiving Father, thank You that You are always with us, even when we try to run from You or from our problems. Help us to remember that Your special promises to us are forever.

Branching Out

1. Build a small stone "pillar" and place it somewhere you will pass often. Talk about a promise from God you would like to remember when you see it.
2. Reread the original covenant promise that God made with Abram in Genesis 12:2 and 15:5-6. What new promises does God make and confirm to Jacob?
3. People try many things to get close to God, including good works, religion, and prayer. What other ways can you think of that people try to reach God? What does God say is the only way to the Father? (see John 14:6)

December 8: *Joseph*

Genesis 45:4-7

Jacob had twelve sons. He loved his youngest son, Joseph, very much and gave him a marvelous colorful robe because he was his favorite. God gave Joseph a marvelous gift as well- special dreams. Some of Joseph's dreams made his eleven older brothers angry and jealous. One day they sold him to slave traders who took their brother to Egypt. Joseph had a hard life- he spent many years in jail for something he didn't do and he was far from his family and home. All the while, God kept giving Joseph special dreams and the ability to explain other people's dreams. Joseph even helped explain the dream of the king of Egypt. From then on, Joseph was put in charge of Pharaoh's entire kingdom! At home, Joseph's family was running out of things to eat and his brothers came to Egypt to buy food. Joseph's brothers didn't know that the person who could help them was the very brother they sold to slave traders years ago. Instead of being mad and punishing his brothers for the wrong things they did, Joseph's heart was full of love and mercy. He forgave his brothers for their sin against him and rescued his entire family from the famine in their land.

God used Joseph to save His chosen people from dying of hunger. Later on, God would send another son- His Son, to feed His people, forgive their sins, and rescue them from death. His heart would also be full of love and mercy.

Father in Heaven, Your plans are always for the good of those who trust You. Thank You for preparing Joseph to save his family, and for sending Jesus to save us from our sins and fill the hunger in our hearts for a Savior. Help us to be quick to forgive and slow to become angry.

 Branching Out

1. Gather canned goods and non-perishable foods and bring them to a local food pantry. Consider volunteering to help prepare and/or serve a meal at a local church or homeless shelter.
2. Think of someone who has hurt your feelings or done something mean or unfair. What would it look like to forgive that person? What happened when Joseph forgave his brothers?
3. Find a colorful shirt or sweater, and act out the story of Joseph and his brothers with your family. You can find more of the story in Genesis 37 and Genesis 42-46.

December 9: *Moses*

Exodus 3:2-7, 10

After the people of God resettled in Egypt, they had many children and their family grew very large. The Pharaoh who was king when Joseph lived had died and the new Pharaoh treated God's people very badly. They became slaves to the Egyptians and cried out to God for help.

Moses was an Israelite who was raised by Pharaoh's daughter in Egypt. One day, while he was taking care of sheep, an angel appeared to Moses in a burning bush. The bush was on fire but it did not burn up. God used the bush to get Moses' attention, and then He spoke to Moses. God told Moses that He remembered the special covenant promises He made to Abraham, Isaac, and Jacob, to look after the people of Israel. God then told Moses that it was his job to tell Pharaoh to let God's people go free. He wanted Moses to lead God's people out of slavery in Egypt and into the Promised Land that God had set aside for them. Moses wasn't sure he could lead the people on his own, but God promised Moses that He would be with him the entire way. God had a plan to rescue His people and he wanted Moses to help Him. Many years later, God would send the perfect Rescuer, Jesus, to set His people free from being slaves to sin just as the Israelites needed to be saved from their slavery to the Egyptians.

Awesome God, You always have a plan! Thank You that You hear us when we pray and cry out to You, and that You are always with us. Help us to always pay attention when You speak to us.

Branching Out

1. Look back in your Bible, or in this book, and recall the covenant promises God made to Abraham, Isaac, and Jacob.
2. God used a burning bush to get Moses' attention. In what ways does God get our attention now?
3. People are still in slavery today all over the world. Take time as a family to pray for their safety and that God would hear their cries and set them free.

December 10: *The Passover Lamb*

Exodus 12:21-23

Moses went to Pharaoh to ask Him to let the Israelites go free, but God had made Pharaoh's heart hard and stubborn. He refused. God sent awful plagues to warn Pharaoh. Water turned into blood. Frogs, gnats, flies, and locusts filled peoples' homes and fields. Livestock died. Everyone's skin was covered with boils. Thunder boomed and hail rained down across the land. Darkness covered the earth. The plagues kept getting worse, and still Pharaoh would not let God's people go. Moses told Pharaoh that God would send one final plague if Pharaoh refused to obey God- the oldest son in each Egyptian family would die, but the Israelites' sons would be safe. God's people were told to kill their best lamb and put some of its blood around the front door of their houses. The Lord would see that the lamb died instead of their sons and He would pass over their house.

All night the Egyptians could be heard crying and screaming as their eldest sons died, but it wasn't until Pharaoh's own son died that he finally let the Israelites leave Egypt. The people of God began a long journey that night as Moses led them out of Egypt and away from slavery. God's people called this night the "Passover" since God passed over their houses when He saw the blood of the lamb on their front door. Many years later God sent Jesus, the Lamb of God, to die in place of His people. His blood shed on the cross set people free from being slaves to sin and hopelessness forever.

God of Justice, You cringe when Your people are held captive. We remember that the blood of Jesus, the Lamb of God, sets us free from sin and death. Help us to live like we are free from the chains of sin, and remind us to pray and fight for the freedom of others.

Branching Out

1. Construct a doorway out of popsicle sticks or construction paper. Use your finger or a paintbrush to spread red paint over the top of your doorframe, like the Israelites did during the Passover.
2. Make a list of the ten plagues in the order they occurred (see Exodus 7-10). Which one do you think was the worst? Why?
3. Visit the website for the International Justice Mission (www.ijm.org) to read more about modern-day slaves, and how you can become involved in advocating for their freedom and praying for justice for their captors.

December 11: *The Ten Commandments*

Exodus 20:1-8, 12-17

As Moses led the people of God through the desert on their journey to the Promised Land, they quickly forgot the amazing things their God had done. God hid them from the Egyptians who chased them as they fled and parted the sea so they could escape to safety. God gave them food from heaven every day and made water flow from a rock, but still they wondered if they could trust God to take care of them. They began making their own rules instead of obeying God's rules.

To remind His people how much He loved them, God called Moses up to a high mountain and gave him the Ten Commandments. These were rules and boundaries to live by, given by God himself. The commandments explained to His people how the world worked best, because God created the world and He created the people who lived in it. God desires to protect His people. He created these boundaries to keep the Israelites and their hearts safe. God wanted His people to love him most of all- more than any other person, thing, or idea. He also told them to always tell the truth, never steal or make pretend gods or statues, and to be thankful for what they had instead of wanting what someone else had. Even though the Israelites promised to obey God's rules all the time, God knew they would never be able to do it on their own. He had a plan to send Someone to be perfect in all the ways they couldn't be. God didn't give His people rules because He thought they would save them or guarantee them a place in heaven. He gave them Jesus for that. God gave His people the commandments because He loved them deeply and He wanted them to know the joy and peace He had designed them for.

Father God, thank You for loving us enough to set boundaries and rules for Your people. Help us to love You more than anything else in this world.

 Branching Out

1. Together with your family, write a list of Ten Family Commandments. What are the most important things to your family?
2. Which commandment is the hardest for you to obey? Why? Which ones is the easiest?
3. Read Matthew 5:21-22, 27-28. What does God care about most as we seek to keep His commandments? Are there some commandments that are more important to keep than others?

December 12: *Joshua*

Joshua 6:15-16, 20

Moses led the Israelites on a very long journey toward a place God had set apart specifically for His people, called the Promised Land. To get to the Promised Land, God's people had to pass through a city called Jericho. Jericho was surrounded by huge walls. These walls were designed to stop people from passing by the city into the land beyond it, but that was exactly where the Israelites needed to go. God's people were scared and they had no idea how they would get past the walls. As always, though, God had a plan. God told Joshua to tell the people to march around the city walls once a day for six days. On the seventh day they were to march around the city seven times, then blow their trumpets and shout as loud as they could. This may have sounded like an odd plan, but God's people trusted Joshua and Joshua trusted God. On the seventh day, after their seventh trip around the city of Jericho, the priests blew a final, long trumpet blast... and the huge walls of that big city crumbled to the ground!

God's people were thankful that He had led them to their new home but before long, they forgot to obey God's rules. They didn't love God with their whole hearts. They fought with one another. They began to worship other gods. They became slaves again and had to leave the Promised Land. Even though His people kept turning away, God would continue to make ways for His people to be close to Him. Eventually, He sent his Son Jesus to be the ultimate and only way to God. Jesus said, "I am the way, the truth, and the life. No one comes to the Father except through me" (John 14:6)

Mighty God, no obstacle is too big for You. Thank You for sending Jesus to be our way to everlasting life with You and for creating a home for us in Heaven that is greater than we can ever imagine.

 Branching Out

1. Using blocks or pillows, build a pretend Jericho, complete with very high walls. Act out the story of Joshua and his army. Be sure to shout as loud as you can when the time comes!
2. Talk about a time when you faced a large obstacle on your way to reaching a goal. How did you overcome it?
3. The Israelites quickly forgot the great things God had done for them after they entered the Promised Land. Do we sometimes forget the good things God has done in our lives? What can we do to remind ourselves of His goodness?

December 13: *Jonah*

Jonah 3:1-5, 10

Jonah was one of God's special messengers. One day, God gave Jonah a very important message to share with the people of Nineveh. God told Jonah to warn the people in Nineveh to stop making evil choices and to worship God instead of idols. Jonah knew the people in Nineveh did bad things. He did not want to go there to tell them that God loved them and wanted to forgive them. Jonah decided to run away from God and His instructions by taking a boat ride to a different town far away from Nineveh.

While he was on the boat, God sent a big storm to get Jonah's attention. The storm was so fierce that Jonah had to jump into the sea to make it stop. Jonah thought he would die in the sea, but God sent a big fish to rescue Jonah from drowning in the water. Jonah stayed inside the fish's belly for three days. It was there that he prayed and told God he was sorry for running from Him. Jonah realized that his plan to run from God wasn't a good plan at all, because God was always with Him. God caused the big fish to spit Jonah out of his belly onto dry land. Jonah then obeyed God. He went to share God's message with the people of Nineveh and they started loving and following God again.

Jonah learned that God is always with us, even when we don't obey Him. He loves us at all times, no matter where we go or what we do. God's love for His people is very strong- stronger even than our sin. He sent many messengers to His people, including his own Son, Jesus. Jesus was God's entire message of love, repentance, and forgiveness in one person.

Wonderful Rescuer, thank You for never leaving us. We want to listen when You are speaking to us. Please show us how to obey quickly, cheerfully, and completely. Help us to share Your message of love and forgiveness with others.

Branching Out

1. What do you think it was like in the fish's belly? What might it have felt like, looked like, smelled like, and sounded like?
2. Jonah tried to run from God. How do we sometimes do that in our own lives? Why does it never work?
3. Ask God if there is someone in your life with whom He would like you to share His message of love and forgiveness. Will you go tell them?

December 14: *Gideon*

Judges 7:20-21

Sometimes, God chooses weak people to do big things so that everyone knows it was God's strength and wisdom that gave them success. That's what happened to Gideon. Gideon was from a small, poor family in a town that was taken over by the Midianites. The Midianites were big, tall, and mean. They bullied God's people by taking their food, ruining their land, and making them leave their homes. One day God sent an angel to tell Gideon that God wanted him to lead an army in battle against the Midianites. Gideon was afraid he couldn't do the job, but God said, "I will be with you" (Judges 6:16).

God gave Gideon instructions for how the little army would conquer their enemy. The men carried torches hidden under clay jars as they snuck up on the town of Midian. They made a circle around the Midianite camp and blew their trumpets, waved their torches, broke their pots, and shouted at the top of their lungs. This made the Midianites so scared that they ran away instead of fighting and Gideon's little army won the battle!

Gideon's victory showed his people that God was strong and mighty, and they began loving God again. They obeyed His commands, got rid of their pretend gods, and worshipped only the One True God. Years later, God would send another small, poor, unlikely leader to rescue His people. He sent His Son, Jesus, as a tiny baby who would lead His people in the battle against sin and darkness...and He too would win!

Most High God, You fight for us and with us in our battles. Just as You were with Gideon, You are always with us. You said in Your Word that when we are weak, You are strong (2 Corinthians 12:10)! Thank You for giving us victory when we trust in You.

Branching Out

1. Take a flashlight, bucket, and horn or pretend trumpet (a kazoo will also work) and practice being in Gideon's army. Use your bucket to hide your "torch" until it is time to surprise the Midianites!
2. Talk about a time when you were asked to do something you felt too small or weak to do. How did God help you through?
3. Make a list of other times in the Bible when God promises to be with a person or people.

December 15: *Ruth*

Ruth 4:13-17

Ruth was a young woman from the city of Moab. Her husband and husband's father and brother died, leaving Ruth and her mother-in-law, Naomi, widowed. Naomi told Ruth to return to her own family to find a new husband, but Ruth clung to Naomi. Showing faithfulness and loyalty, she said, "Where you go I will go, and where you stay I will stay. Your people will be my people and your God my God" (Ruth 1: 16).

Ruth and Naomi traveled to the town of Bethlehem just as the barley harvest had begun. Ruth went to the fields each day to collect the harvesters' leftovers so she and Naomi would have food to eat. The owner of the field was a man named Boaz, who was a relative of Naomi's. Boaz was a kind man who made sure Ruth had lots of leftovers to bring home. Boaz eventually took Ruth to be his wife, promising to take care of her and Naomi and so redeem them from being widowed and alone. Ruth and Boaz had a son together. Through their son, their descendants included David, a great king over Israel, and Jesus, the great King of Kings. God planned for Boaz to redeem Ruth in Bethlehem. In that same city, the King of Kings would be born to redeem all of God's people back to Himself.

God in Heaven, thank You for sending Your Son Jesus to guard our hearts and redeem us from sin. Help us to join You in looking after "orphans and widows in their distress" (James 1:27).

Branching Out

1. Ruth gleaned leftover barley from Boaz's fields. Prepare a recipe using barley, and discuss how it tastes. Let everyone in the family feel some of the barley before and after it's been cooked.
2. Visit or send a card to someone you know who has lost their husband or wife. You may also consider inviting them to share a meal with your family.
3. As a family, consider sponsoring a child through an organization such as Compassion International (www.compassion.com) or World Vision (www.worldvision.org).

December 16: *Samuel*

1 Samuel 3:19-21   1 Samuel 12:19-24

From the time Samuel was a young boy, God had chosen him to be one of His prophets. A prophet hears from God and shares God's message with the people. Samuel listened and obeyed the Lord's calling for his life. He proclaimed to God's people that a true King was coming who would rule over every earthly king. When God's people entered their new land they wanted a new king that they could see, hear, and touch. Even though they had a God who was kind and fair as He looked out for their needs and even though they had a history of being ruled by leaders who did not take good care of them, the people of Israel still wanted an earthly king. God heard His people and gave them a king named Saul, but Saul neither loved God, nor followed His commands.

God told Samuel to go to Bethlehem to find the new king that God had chosen to care for and lead His people. God had chosen David, an earthly man who loved God with his whole heart. Many years later a relative of David would be born in the same city of Bethlehem. God would choose this man, His Son Jesus, to be the King of Kings. The prophet Isaiah said that this King's kingdom would have "no end" (Isaiah 9:7), and Daniel described that "the God of heaven will set up a kingdom that will never be destroyed, nor will it be left to another people. It will crush all those kingdoms and bring them to an end, but it will itself endure forever" (Daniel 2:44).

Everlasting God, You know just what Your people need. Help us to trust and pray for those You put in authority over us, because You are wise and good.

 Branching Out

1. Make a list of people that God has put in positions of leadership and authority over you. Take time as a family to pray for God's wisdom and protection for each of these people. "I urge, then, first of all, that petitions, prayers, intercession and thanksgiving be made for all people- for kings and all those in authority, that we may live peaceful and quiet lives in all godliness and holiness. This is good, and pleases God our Savior..." (1 Timothy 2:1-4)

2. Write a letter to one of these people and tell them how you are praying for them.

3. Samuel encouraged God's people to serve the Lord and "consider what great things He has done..." (1 Samuel 12:24). As a family, spend time recalling and thanking God for the great things He has done for you over the past year.

December 17: *David*

1 Samuel 16:11-13

God has big plans for our lives even when we are still young. He sees what is in our hearts and what kind of person we will grow up to be. God knew that there was a wise and mighty king inside the little shepherd boy David. He saw that David's heart was brave and full of love for God and for people, which is why God told Samuel to go to Bethlehem to find the new king. Samuel went to the house of a man named Jesse and looked at all of his sons. When he met Jesse's youngest son, David, the Lord told Samuel that this boy would be the new king. Even though he was just a boy, Samuel anointed David (by pouring oil on his head) to show that he was the one God had chosen to be king.

David started out as a shepherd of animals, but God called him to be a shepherd of people. God chose David to be a king and to lead His people like a shepherd leads and takes care of sheep: "...And the Lord said to you, 'You will shepherd my people Israel, and you will become their ruler'" (2 Samuel 5:2). God used David to get His special peoples' hearts ready for another king, also called the (Good) Shepherd. This Good Shepherd, a man from David's family tree, would lay down His life for His sheep- the people of God. Jesus said, "I am the good shepherd; I know my sheep and my sheep know me – just as the Father knows me and I know the Father – and I lay down my life for the sheep" (John 10:14-15).

Gracious Father, help our hearts to be full of love for You and for people like David's was. Thank You for giving us a Shepherd who takes good care of us.

Branching Out

1. Visit a live nativity (or local petting zoo) in your town to see, feel, and hear what live sheep are like.
2. List several ways a shepherd takes care of his sheep. How is that similar to the ways that Jesus, the Good Shepherd, cares for us? (see John 10:1-18 and 1 Peter 2:25)
3. David was the youngest of his brothers, and just a boy when Samuel first anointed him as God's chosen king. How do you think David felt when that happened? How might you feel if you were in his place?

1 Kings 18:38-39

David's son Solomon became king after David's death. At this time, the kingdom was beginning to fall apart. Elijah was God's special messenger at the time when Israel started to worship false gods and forget about the One True God. When Elijah was alive, there was famine and drought in the land. Most of God's people were worshipping and serving idols, which are images of false gods, in hopes that the famine and drought would end. Elijah did not worship idols. He remembered the One True God and tried to remind the people of the many promises God made to them (and kept!) in the past. To prove how awesome and worthy his God was, Elijah and the prophets of Baal, a false god, had a contest. They both built stone altars, sacrificed a bull, and prayed to their God/god to send fire to the altar. The prophets of Baal chanted and danced all day and, not surprisingly, nothing happened. When Elijah prayed, however, God immediately sent fire to the altar to prove His power and might and to remind His people that He was the only God they should worship.

The Bible says that "those who cling to worthless idols turn away from God's love for them" (Jonah 2:8). Just like the people of God experienced over and over, it is easy for us to forget about God's perfect love for us and to give the love in our hearts to things instead of to God. God's love for us is never-ending. Even when His people are far from Him and make bad choices, God does amazing things to turn our attention and our hearts back towards Him. "This is love: not that we loved God, but that he loved us and sent his Son as an atoning sacrifice for our sins" (1 John 4:10).

Awesome God, You are the Lord and the One True God. Thank You for loving us by sending Your Son to forgive our sins. Help us to worship only You and not cling to or give our love to worthless idols.

Branching Out

1. Memorize 1 John 4:10.
2. Atonement can be thought of as "at-one-ment," or being "at one" with someone. How did Jesus' sacrifice make us "at one" with God?
3. What things can become idols in our own lives? List some things that we can be tempted to trust in, give our love and attention to, or value more than God.

December 19: *Jeremiah*

Jeremiah 23:5-6   2 Chronicles 36:15-16, 20-21

Once again, God's people returned to worshipping idols and disobeying God until, as it says, "there (was) no remedy" (Jeremiah 36:16). The kingdom of Israel had been destroyed and the remnant of God's people, called Judah, were again heading into exile – this time in Babylon. In that time God chose a young man named Jeremiah to be His prophet. The Lord told Jeremiah that He had set him apart to be His prophet before he was even born. Jeremiah was nervous and told God that he was too young to do what God was calling him to do. The Lord told Jeremiah not to be afraid and reminded him that He would be with him and would rescue him always. Then God reached out and touched Jeremiah's mouth to show that He had put His words in Jeremiah's mouth for him to share with the people.

God sent Jeremiah to tell His people how His heart was broken that they had again returned to worshipping idols. He also wanted Jeremiah to tell them that this would not be the end. Although they would experience sadness, death, and sickness, and would cry many tears, God had a plan for the remnant of Israel to return to their land once again. There, they would learn to receive God's comfort and to be satisfied with God's blessings for them. God would establish a new covenant with the Israelites (Jeremiah 31:33-34) and everyone would know the One True God.

Jeremiah told God's people that He promised to raise up a new leader for them- a branch of the root of David and Jesse's family, to rule over the people. This "righteous Branch" is Jesus, who was born around 600 years after the Israelites' exile in Babylon. Through Jesus, a new covenant was established. God's relationship with His people changed from laws to love, although many would say it was based on love all along.

Righteous One, You forgive Your people even when they break Your heart. Help our hearts to be filled and satisfied by You only so that there is no room for idols. Thank you for sending Jesus to be our righteous Leader and King.

Branching Out

1. Go outside and find a tree (or a picture of a tree) with many branches. Talk about how the branches are connected to the trunk and roots of the tree.
2. What does it mean to be satisfied with God's blessings?
3. Look up the meaning of the word "righteous." Talk with your family about what it looks like to live "righteously." Why is it important to have leaders that are righteous?

Habakkuk 2:1, 3

Habakkuk was another prophet of God. He was honest and did not pretend or hide his feelings when he talked with God. Habakkuk's book in the Bible begins with him crying out to the Lord, which means that Habakkuk was distressed and looking to God for help. Throughout the Bible God tells those who believe in Him to cry out to Him in times of trouble: "...call on me in the day of trouble; I will deliver you, and you will honor me" (Psalm 50:15). Habakkuk knew that God hears each of us when we share our troubles and hurts with Him in prayer, and he reminds us to trust God to heal our broken places, even when it takes a long time. Habakkuk also knew that God doesn't need or want us to pretend with Him. Habakkuk acted as a watchman for God's people as he patiently waited, with a heart full of faith, for God to answer their prayer to send someone to end the violence against Israel and bring them everlasting peace.

"You know the message God sent to the people of Israel, announcing the good news of peace through Jesus Christ, who is Lord of all" (Acts 10:36). That peace would be a person- Jesus, our Prince of Peace. "For unto us a child is born, to us a son is given, and the government will be on his shoulders. And he will be called Wonderful Counselor, Mighty God, Everlasting Father, Prince of Peace" (Isaiah 9:6).

Mighty God, sometimes we have to wait a long time for You to answer our prayers. Help us to be honest when we pray and to wait well and faithfully like Habakkuk.

Branching Out

1. Waiting can be hard. What things do we sometimes need to wait for?
2. Describe a time when you had to wait a long time for God to answer a prayer. Is there something you are praying about right now that you are still waiting for God to answer? How can we remain faithful as we wait?
3. Take time as a family to pray for peace in our lives and in our world. Are there certain people or places you can think of that especially need the Prince of Peace right now?

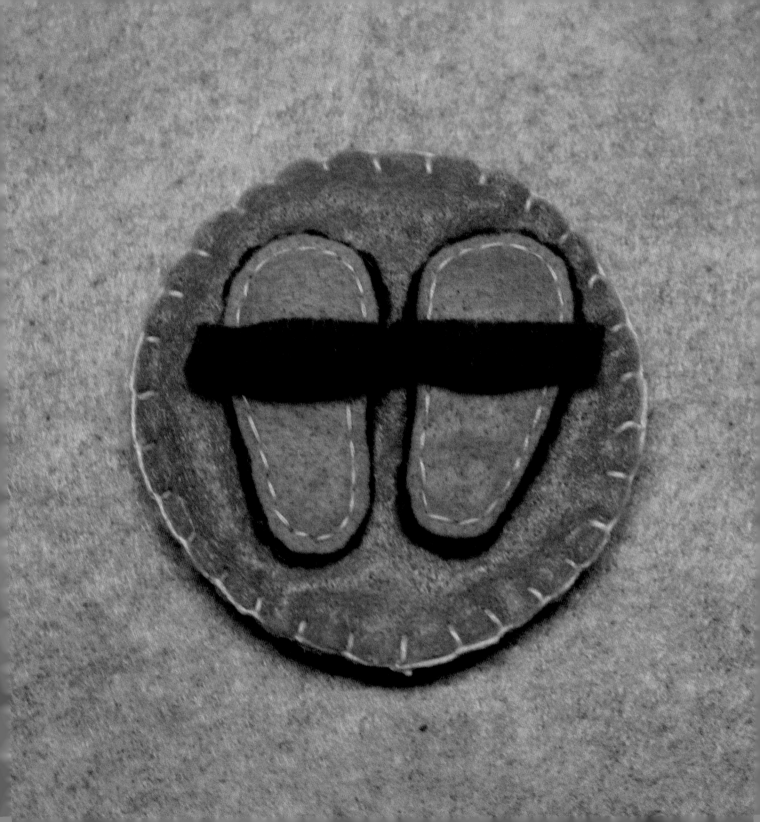

Matthew 3:1-3, 11   John 1:6-8

Many years passed from the Israelites' exile and return to worshipping idols. During that time, God's people suffered under various rulers that were unkind to them. The Israelites thought God might have forgotten about them, but He hadn't. He was waiting for just the right time to send His Son Jesus to rescue His people. After years and years of silence, God sent another messenger to His people. God chose a man named John to tell His people that Jesus was the promised Messiah and that He was coming soon. John helped the Israelites get their hearts ready to meet Jesus by explaining who Jesus was and by baptizing them in the river. John baptized many people, including Jesus himself! Being baptized meant that John lowered a person in and out of water to show that they were starting a new life. This new life started with choosing God's way as right, turning away from their sin, and believing that Jesus was the Messiah and the Son of the Living God. Having their body cleansed with water represented that their hearts had been cleansed by their new faith in God.

John shared that Jesus was the light God had sent to earth so people could see and know the One True God. The light of Jesus' life would shine on the darkness in peoples' hearts. When they confessed their sins, Jesus would rescue them from their wrongdoing and shame. John knew that Jesus was mightier than any man who had ever lived on earth. John wasn't even worthy to carry Jesus' sandals because Jesus' holiness made Him so wonderful.

Loving God, thank You for Your gift of baptism and for sending John to announce Jesus' coming. Prepare our own hearts to be ready to meet Jesus when He comes again.

Branching Out

1. Place several scoops of dirt (or black paint) inside a glass jar with a tight fitting lid, to represent what our hearts look like when we sin. We can't get the "sin" or dirt out on our own, no matter how hard we scrub the outside. When we trust Jesus and give our lives to Him, the inside of our heart is made clean (wash dirt from inside jar). Baptism shows on the outside how our hearts have been cleansed on the inside, by Jesus.

2. What does the Bible say about baptism? (See John 1:33, John 3:5, Acts 2:38, Romans 6:4, Galatians 3:27, 1 Peter 3:21, etc.)

3. In what ways is the physical act of baptism also a visual representation of Christ's burial and resurrection?

Luke 1:26-33

Mary was a young Jewish girl engaged to a man named Joseph, who was a descendant of King David. One day, one of God's messengers visited Mary to tell her that God had a special job for her. He needed a home on earth for His son Jesus and had chosen Mary to be Jesus' earthly mother. God was pleased with Mary's pure heart and knew she would be the kind of mother His Son needed- wise, smart, strong, and someone who trusted God completely. God reminded Mary that He would always be with her and Mary trusted God beyond what her eyes could see. She joyfully welcomed the baby that God placed inside her through the Holy Spirit. Mary promised God to be His servant and to do the job He had given her with a faith-filled heart. "'I am the Lord's servant,' Mary answered. 'May your word to me be fulfilled.'" (Luke 1:38).

God's decision to choose Mary to become the mother of Jesus was even more special because it had been spoken of many years earlier by the prophet Isaiah: "Therefore the Lord himself will give you a sign: The virgin will conceive and give birth to a son, and will call him Immanuel." (Isaiah 7:14), which means "God with us" (Matthew 1:22). Mary's special job and Jesus her special Son were all part of God's great plan to give a sign to His people of His faithful and never-ending love for them. The words spoken by Isaiah long ago were fulfilled through Jesus' coming. His birth completed God's promises to send a sign to His people through a miraculous birth and to remain near His people as "God with us."

Lord God, You are and always will be Emmanuel, God with us. Thank You for choosing Mary to be the earthly mother of Your Son, Jesus. Help us to be Your servants, with joy-filled hearts, as we live out Your promises to us.

Branching Out

1. Make an angel out of paper and craft supplies to remind you of the angel that visited Mary.

2. Together as a family, sing or listen to the song "O Come, O Come Emmanuel" (translated by John Mason Neale in 1854). Listen for other references to the coming Messiah in the verses of this song: Emmanuel (Isaiah 7:14), Rod (Branch) of Jesse (Isaiah 11:1, 11:10), Dayspring (Morning Star) (Numbers 24:17).

3. God promised Mary that He would be with her as she did the job He gave her. He promises that to us too in Mathew 28:20. What does this mean when we are asked to do difficult things?

December 23: *Joseph*

Matthew 1:18-25

God knew that in addition to an earthly mother, Jesus would also need an earthly father. He chose a man named Joseph who was engaged to be married to Mary. Joseph trusted God, but he didn't understand at first that Mary's baby had come from God. Still, Joseph set out to protect Mary's dignity and shield her from disgrace, much as his earthly son Jesus did years later when He died on the cross for our sins and freed us from shame.

God sent an angel to Joseph to help him understand God's plan for sending His Son Jesus to earth as a baby. Joseph realized that he and Mary had a special role to play in God's plan to send a Savior to the world. He shows his deep trust in God and his strong love for Mary by becoming Mary's husband and raising God's Son together. Joseph was a carpenter. In his workshop he taught Jesus many things about woodworking and about the character of God as they worked together during Jesus' childhood. Jesus was able to teach others about the Father-heart of God, likely because of the example of fatherhood that Joseph showed to Him. Jesus taught that the Father knows our needs (Matthew 6:8), forgives (6:14), provides for His children (6:26), gives good gifts (7:11), cares (10:29), and knows His Son (11:27).

Our Father in Heaven, You know our needs and provide well for us. Help us to hear Your voice, trust what You say, and follow Your directions. Thank You that we all have important parts to play in Your magnificent story.

Branching Out

1. Name three things you have learned from your earthly father or a father-figure in your life.
2. In the time when Joseph and Mary lived, a young woman who was pregnant and unmarried could have been publicly shamed or even stoned as an adultress. In what ways did Joseph act righteously in his response to Mary's announcement that she was expecting a baby?
3. Read God's promise to David through the prophet Nathan in 2 Samuel 7:12-16, and the following verses: Psalm 132:11, Luke 1:32-33, Luke 2:4, Acts 13:22-23, and Revelation 22:16. What about Joseph's family lineage was a specific fulfillment of Old Testament prophecy about the coming Messiah?

Luke 2:1-20

While Mary and Joseph were expecting their baby, a ruler named Caesar Augustus was conducting a census. In order to count each person, he required everyone to return to their hometown. It took Mary and Joseph several days to journey back to Joseph's hometown of Bethlehem. Many important things happened in this town- Boaz and Ruth lived there with their son Obed. Obed's son Jesse and Jesse's son David lived there as well. The prophet Micah spoke that the ruler over Israel would also come from Bethlehem: "But you, Bethlehem Ephrathah, though you are small among the clans of Judah, out of you will come for me one who will be ruler over Israel, whose origins are from old, from ancient times. Therefore Israel will be abandoned until the time when she who is in labor bears a son, and the rest of his brothers return to join the Israelites. He will stand and shepherd his flock in the strength of the Lord, in the majesty of the name of the Lord his God. And they will live securely, for then his greatness will reach to the ends of the earth. And he will be our peace..." (Micah 5:2-5). God planned the place of Jesus' birth long before it took place.

The journey to Bethlehem was difficult and took many days. When Mary and Joseph arrived, it was time for Mary to give birth, but all of the places to stay in town were full. Joseph eventually found room in a place where animals were kept and made a place for Mary to have her baby. On a dark winter night, likely next to donkeys and sheep, the Savior of the world was born. God hung a bright star in the sky that night to tell everyone that the Light of the World had come to earth. Shepherds and wise men followed this star to find the Messiah they had long been waiting for.

Wonderful God, You were a proud Father the night Your Son was born! Thank You for sending the Light of the World to pierce the darkness in our hearts.

Branching Out

1. What journeys have you taken this year? Look through pictures, scrapbooks, and videos and remember together.
2. Ask your parents to tell you about the day you were born. Where were you born? Who was there? How did your parents know it was time?
3. The shepherds and wise men brought gifts to baby Jesus. What gifts would you have given Him? What gifts can you give God this year?

December 25: *Jesus*

Hebrews 1:1-2, 3

Today we celebrate the arrival of God's Son, Jesus, and the fulfillment of His promise to send a Savior who would redeem all people back to God the Father. God's heart grieved for His people when sin entered the world through Adam and Eve. God remained with His people, even when they wandered away from Him. God kept loving them and pursuing a relationship with His people when they gave their love to other gods. God was faithful to send the Rescuer He promised, and today we celebrate the arrival of that promise. Jesus shows us the depth of God's love for us- His faithful, persistent, never-ending, sacrificial love to send His beloved Son to a world full of sin and to a people who would forget their God again and again.

Jesus ... the Good Shepherd ... Messiah ... Light of the World ... Prince of Peace ... Rescuer ... Emmanuel ... God with us.

Jesus came to earth as a baby that needed to be held, loved, and touched, and He would continue to love and reach out to all people as He grew into a man. Through His death and resurrection, we can be reconciled with God and forgiven of our sins. Jesus is and forever will be the most wonderful and life-changing gift we can ever receive. Joy to the world, the Lord is come!

Glorious One, You loved the world so much that You sent Your one and only Son to give eternal life to everyone who believes. Your faithfulness and glory are shown in Jesus Himself. May we also reflect Your glory in our lives. Amen.

Branching Out

1. Bake a cake together in honor of Jesus' birthday!
2. What is your favorite part of the Christmas story? Recount all the ways you can remember that Jesus' birth was hinted at in the stories you've read this Advent season.
3. Gather as a family and sing or listen to your favorite Christmas hymns together.

Appendix A: *Bible Verses*

December 1: The Jesse Tree

A shoot will come up from the stump of Jesse; from his roots a Branch will bear fruit. The Spirit of the Lord will rest on him- the Spirit of wisdom and of understanding, the Spirit of counsel and of might, the Spirit of the knowledge and fear of the Lord...

Isaiah 11:1-2

December 2: Creation

In the beginning God created the heavens and the earth...God created mankind in his own image, in the image of God he created them; male and female he created them...God saw all that he had made, and it was very good...

Genesis 1:1, 27, 31

December 3: Adam and Eve

The man said, "The woman you put here with me – she gave me some fruit from the tree, and I ate it." Then the Lord God said to the woman, "What is this you have done?" The woman said, "The serpent deceived me, and I ate."

Genesis 3: 12-13

We all, like sheep, have gone astray, each of us has turned to our own way; and the Lord has laid on him the iniquity of us all.

Isaiah 53:6

December 4: Noah

I am going to bring floodwaters on the earth to destroy all life under the heavens, every creature that has the breath of life in it. Everything on earth will perish. But I will establish my covenant with you, and you will enter the ark- you and your sons and your wife and your sons' wives with you. You are to bring into the ark two of all living creatures, male and female, to keep them alive with you.

Genesis 6: 17-19

...I establish my covenant with you: Never again will all life be destroyed by the waters of a flood; never again will there be a flood to destroy the earth." And God said, "This is a sign of the covenant I am making between me and you and every living creature with you, a covenant for all generations to come: I have set my rainbow in the clouds, and it will be the sign of the covenant between me and the earth.

Genesis 9: 11-13

December 5: Abraham

I will make you into a great nation, and I will bless you; I will make your name great, and you will be a blessing.

Genesis 12:2

And he took him outside and said, "Look up at the sky and count the stars- if indeed you can count them." Then he said to him, "So shall your offspring be." Abraham believed the Lord, and he credited it to him as righteousness.

Genesis 15:5-6

December 6: Isaac

Abraham answered, "God himself will provide the lamb for the burnt offering, my son." And the two of them went on together. When they reached the place God had told them about, Abraham built an altar there and arranged the wood on it. He bound his son Isaac and laid him on the altar, on top of the wood. Then he reached out his hand and took the knife to slay his son. But the angel of the Lord called out to him from , "Abraham! Abraham!" "Here I am," he replied. "Do not lay a hand on the boy," he said. "Do not do anything to him. Now I know that you fear God, because you have not withheld from me your son, your only son." Abraham looked up and there in a thicket he saw a ram caught by its horns. He went over and took the ram and sacrificed it as a burnt offering instead of his son.

Genesis 22:8-13

December 7: Jacob

He had a dream in which he saw a stairway resting on the earth, with its top reaching to heaven, and the angels of God were ascending and descending on it. There above it stood the Lord, and he said: 'I am the Lord, the God of your father Abraham and the God of Isaac. I will give you and your descendants the land on which you are lying. Your descendants will be like the dust of the earth, and you will spread out to the west and to the east, to the north and to the south. All peoples on earth will be blessed through you and your offspring. I am with you and will watch over you wherever you go, and I will bring you back to this land. I will not leave you until I have done what I have promised you.

Genesis 28:12-15

December 8: Joseph

Then Joseph said to his brothers, "Come close to me." When they had done so, he said, "I am your brother Joseph, the one you sold into Egypt! And now, do not be distressed and do not be angry with yourselves for selling me here, because it was to save lives that God sent me ahead of you. For two years now there has been famine in the land, and for the next five years there will be no plowing and reaping. But God sent me ahead of you to preserve a remnant on earth and to save your lives by a great deliverance."

Genesis 45:4-7

December 9: Moses

The angel of the Lord appeared to him in flames of fire from within a bush. Moses saw that though the bush was on fire it did not burn up. So Moses thought, "I will go over and see this strange sight-why the bush does not burn up." When the Lord saw that he had gone over to look, God called to him from within the bush, "Moses! Moses!" And Moses said, "Here I am." "Do not come any closer," God said. "Take off your sandals, for the place where you are standing is holy ground." Then he said, "I am the God of your father, the God of Abraham, the God of Isaac, and the God of Jacob." At this, Moses hid his face, because he was afraid to look at God. The Lord said, "I have indeed seen the misery of my people in Egypt. I have heard them crying out because of their slave drivers, and I am concerned about their suffering...So now, go. I am sending you to Pharaoh to bring my people the Israelites out of Egypt."

Exodus 3:2-7,10

December 10: The Passover Lamb

Then Moses summoned all the elders of Israel and said to them, "Go at once and select the animals for your families and slaughter the Passover lamb. Take a bunch of hyssop, dip it into the blood in the basin and put some of the blood on the top and on both sides of the doorframe. None of you shall go out of the door of your house until morning. When the Lord goes through the land to strike down the Egyptians, he will see the blood on the top and sides of the doorframe and will pass over that doorway, and he will not permit the destroyer to enter your houses and strike you down."

Exodus 12:21-23

December 11: The Ten Commandments

And God spoke all these words: "I am the Lord your God, who brought you out of Egypt, out of the land of slavery. You shall have no other gods before me. You shall not make yourself an image in the form of anything in heaven above or on the earth beneath or in waters below. You shall not bow down to them or worship them; for I, the Lord your God, am a jealous God, punishing the children for the sin of the parents to the third and fourth generation of those who hate me, but showing love to a thousand generations of those who love me and keep my commandments.

You shall not misuse the name of the Lord your God, for the Lord will not hold anyone guiltless who misuses his name. Remember the Sabbath day by keeping it holy. Six days you shall labor and do all your work, but the seventh day is a sabbath to the Lord your God...

Honor your father and your mother, so that you may live long in the land your God is giving you.

You shall not murder. You shall not commit adultery. You shall not steal. You shall not give false testimony against your neighbor. You shall not covet your neighbor's house. You shall not covet your neighbor's wife, or his male or female servant, his ox or donkey, or anything that belongs to your neighbor."

Exodus 20:1-8, 12-17

December 12: Joshua

On the seventh day, they got up at daybreak and marched around the city seven times in the same manner, except on that day they circled the city seven times. The seventh time around, when the priests sounded the trumpet blast, Joshua commanded the army, "Shout! For the Lord has given you the city!"... When the trumpets sounded, the army shouted, and at the sound of the trumpet, when the men gave a loud shout, the wall collapsed; so everyone charged straight in, and they took the city.

Joshua 6:15-16, 20

December 13: Jonah

Then the word of the Lord came to Jonah a second time: "Go to the great city of Nineveh and proclaim to it the message I give you." Jonah obeyed the word of the Lord and went to Nineveh. Now Nineveh was a very large city; it took three days to go through it. Jonah began by going a day's journey into the city, proclaiming, "Forty more days and Nineveh will be overthrown." The Ninevites believed God. A fast was proclaimed, and all of them, from the greatest to the least, put on sackcloth... When God saw what they did and how they turned from their evil ways, he relented and did not bring on them the destruction he had threatened.

Jonah 3:1-5, 10

December 14: Gideon

The three companies blew the trumpets and smashed the jars. Grasping the torches in their left hands and holding in their right hands the trumpets they were to blow, they shouted, "A sword for the Lord and for Gideon!" While each man held his position around the camp, all the Midianites ran, crying out as they fled.

Judges 7:20-21

December 15: Ruth

So Boaz took Ruth and she became his wife. When he made love to her, the Lord enabled her to conceive, and she gave birth to a son. The woman said to Naomi: "Praise be to the Lord, who this day has not left you without a guardian-redeemer. May he become famous throughout Israel! He will renew your life and sustain you in your old age. For your daughter-in-law, who loves you and who is better to you than seven sons, has given him birth." Then Naomi took the child in her arms and cared for him. The women living there said, "Naomi has a son!" And they named him Obed. He was the father of Jesse, the father of David.

Ruth 4:13-17

December 16: Samuel

The Lord was with Samuel as he grew up, and he let none of Samuel's words fall to the ground. And all Israel from Dan to Beersheba recognized that Samuel was attested as a prophet of the Lord. The Lord continued to appear at Shiloh, and there he revealed himself to Samuel through his word.

1 Samuel 3:19-21

The people all said to Samuel, "Pray to the Lord your God for your servants so that we will not die, for we have added to all our other sins the evil of asking for a king." "Do not be afraid," Samuel replied. "You have done all this evil; yet do not turn away from the Lord, but serve the Lord with all your heart. Do not turn away after useless idols. They can do you no good, nor can they rescue you, because they are useless. For the sake of his great name the Lord will not reject his people, because the Lord was pleased to make you his own. As for me, far be it from me that I should sin against the Lord by failing to pray for you. And I will teach you the way that is good and right. But be sure to fear the Lord and serve him faithfully with all your heart; consider what great things he has done for you"

1 Samuel 12:19-24

December 17: David

So he asked Jesse, "Are these all the sons you have?" "There is still the youngest," Jesse answered. "He is tending the sheep." Samuel said, "Send for him; we will not sit down until he arrives." So he sent for him and had him brought in. He was glowing with health and had a fine appearance and handsome features. Then the Lord said, "Rise and anoint him; this is the one." So Samuel took the horn of oil and anointed him in the presence of his brothers, and from that day on the Spirit of the Lord came powerfully upon David...

1 Samuel 16: 11-13

December 18: Elijah

Then the fire of the Lord fell and burned up the sacrifice, the wood, the stones and the soil, and also licked up the water in the trench. When all the people saw this, they fell prostrate and cried, "The Lord- he is God! The Lord – he is God!"

1 Kings 18:38-39

December 19: Jeremiah

"The days are coming," declares the Lord, "when I will raise up for David a righteous Branch, a King who will reign wisely and do what is just and right in the land. In his days Judah will be saved and Israel will live in safety. This is the name by which he will be called: The Lord Our Righteous Savior."

Jeremiah 23:5-6

The Lord, the God of their ancestors, sent word to them through his messengers again and again, because he had pity on his people and on his dwelling place. But they mocked God's messengers, despised his words and scoffed at his prophets until the wrath of the Lord was aroused against his people and there was no remedy... He carried into exile to Babylon the remnant, who escaped from the sword, and they became servants to him and his successors until the kingdom of Persia came to power. The land enjoyed its sabbath rests; all the time of its desolation it rested, until the seventy years were completed in fulfillment of the word of the Lord spoken by Jeremiah.

2 Chronicles 36: 15-16, 20-21

December 20: Habakkuk

I will stand at my watch and station myself on the ramparts; I will look to see what he will say to me...For the revelation awaits an appointed time; it speaks of the end and will not prove false. Though it linger, wait for it; it will certainly come and will not delay.

Habakkuk 2:1, 3

December 21: John the Baptist

In those days John the Baptist came, preaching in the wilderness of Judea and saying, 'Repent, for the kingdom of heaven has come near.' This is he who was spoken of through the prophet Isaiah: "A voice of one calling in the wilderness, 'Prepare the way for the Lord, make straight paths for him'"... "I baptize you with water for repentance. But after me comes one who is more powerful than I, whose sandals I am not worthy to carry. He will baptize you with the Holy Spirit and fire."

Matthew 3:1-3, 11

There was a man sent from God whose name was John. He came as a witness to testify concerning that light, so that through him all might believe. He himself was not the light; he came only as a witness to the light.

John 1:6-8

December 22: Mary

In the sixth month of Elizabeth's pregnancy, God sent the angel Gabriel to Nazareth, a town in Galilee, to a virgin pledged to be married to a man named Joseph, a descendant of David. The virgin's name was Mary. The angel went to her and said, "Greetings, you who are highly favored! The Lord is with you." Mary was greatly troubled at his words and wondered what kind of greeting this might be. But the angel said to her, "Do not be afraid, Mary; you have found favor with God. You will conceive and give birth to a son, and you are to call him Jesus. He will be great and will be called the Son of the Most High. The Lord God will give him the throne of his father David, and he will reign over Jacob's descendants forever; his kingdom will never end."

Luke 1:26-33

December 23: Joseph

This is how the birth of Jesus the Messiah came about: His mother Mary was pledged to be married to Joseph, but before they came together, she was found to be pregnant through the Holy Spirit. Because Joseph her husband was faithful to the law, and yet did not want to expose her to public disgrace, he had in mind to divorce her quietly. But after he had considered this, an angel of the Lord appeared to him in a dream and said, "Joseph son of David, do not be afraid to take Mary home as your wife, because what is conceived in her is from the Holy Spirit. She will give birth to a son, and you are to give him the name Jesus, because he will save his people from their sins." All this took place to fulfill what the Lord had said through the prophet: "The virgin will conceive and give birth to a son, and they will call him Immanuel" (which means "God with us"). When Joseph woke up, he did what the angel of the Lord had commanded him and took Mary home as his wife. But he did not consummate their marriage until she gave birth to a son. And he gave him the name Jesus.

Matthew 1:18-25

December 24: Bethlehem

In those days Caesar Augustus issued a decree that a census should be taken of the entire Roman world. (This was the first census that took place while Quirinius was governor of Syria.) And everyone went to their own town to register. So Joseph also went up from the town of Nazareth in Galilee to Judea, to Bethlehem the town of David, because he belonged to the house and line of David. He went there to register with Mary, who was pledged to be married to him and was expecting a child. While they were there, the time came for the baby to be born, and she gave birth to her firstborn, a son. She wrapped him in cloths and placed him in a manger, because there was no guest room available for them. And there were shepherds living out in the fields nearby, keeping watch over their flocks at night. An angel of the Lord appeared to them, and the glory of the Lord shone around them, and they were terrified. But the angel said to them, "Do not be afraid. I bring you good news that will cause great joy for all the people. Today in the town of David a Savior has been born to you; he is the Messiah, the Lord. This will be a sign to you: You will find a baby wrapped in cloths and lying in a manger." Suddenly a great company of the heavenly host appeared with the angel, praising God and saying, "Glory to God in the highest heaven, and on earth peace to those on whom his favor rests." When the angels had left them and gone into heaven, the shepherds said to one another, "Let's go to Bethlehem and see this thing that has happened, which the Lord has told us about." So they hurried off and found Mary and Joseph, and the baby, who was lying in the manger. When they had seen him, they spread the word concerning what had been told them about this child, and all who heard it were amazed at what the shepherds said to them. But Mary treasured up all these things and pondered them in her heart. The shepherds returned, glorifying and praising God for all the things they had heard and seen, which were just as they had been told.
Luke 2:1-20

December 25: Jesus

Long ago God spoke many times and in many ways through the prophets. And now in these final days, he has spoken to us through his Son...The Son radiates God's own glory and expresses the very character of God...
Hebrews 1:1-2,3

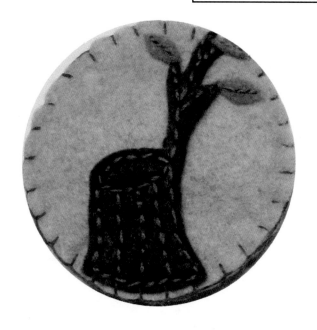

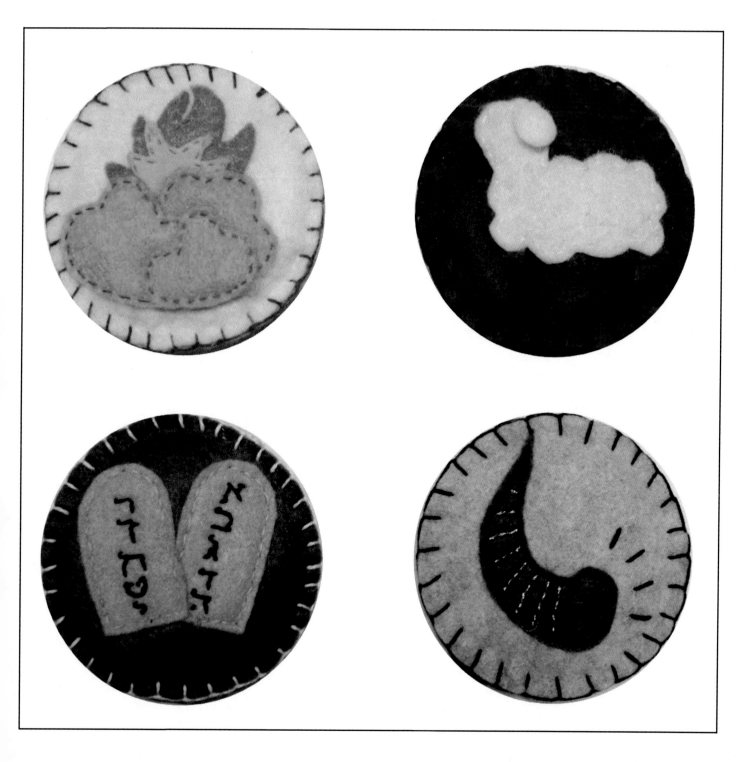

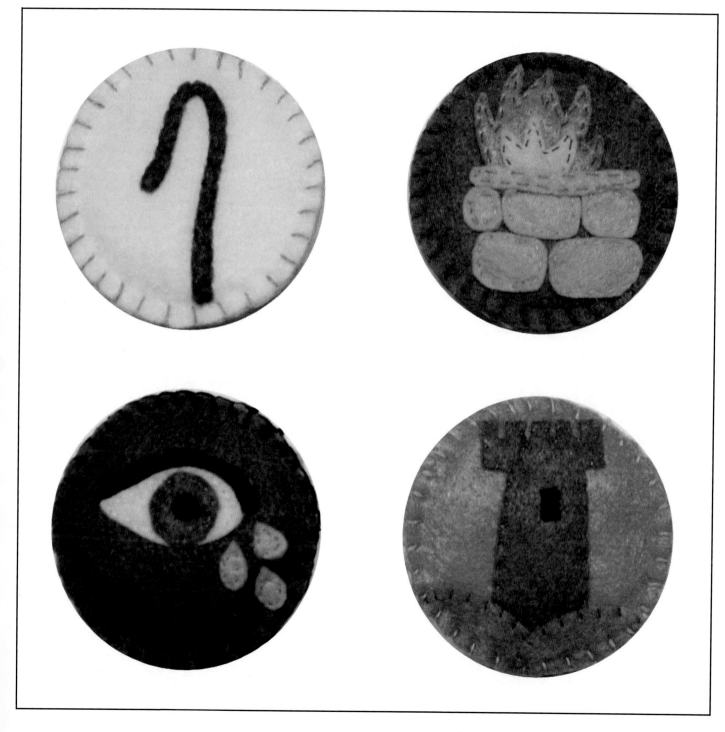

Made in the USA
Las Vegas, NV
20 October 2022

57708776R00050